A

COMPLETE
GUIDE

To

INFLUENCER MARKETING

By

Hope Ofobike

Table of Contents

Introduction

Marketing is the most effective way an entrepreneur can move up the ladder. Platforms, branding, speaking the language of the audience, and figuring out the best marketing strategies are useful for the target consumers can be challenging.It is time to experiment with new ideas if you feel overwhelmed. Influencer marketing is a smart way to boost the bottom line and ROI of your brand.

Chapter One

What is influencer marketing?

Influencer marketing is the practice whereby a group of people markets certain products or services to others whom they must 'influence.' It starts off with the identification and building of relationships with the 'influential individuals' that have the natural ability to persuade and convert prospective buyers into making quick purchase decisions.

Some major influencers in society are bloggers, industry analysts, journalists, and public figures. For example, a revered celebrity may visit a perfume store and post it online. When his or her followers view the post, they have more exposure to the brand. It is at this point that the influence sets in because such followers will nurture the urge to own similar brands. From Cialdini's Six Principles of Persuasion, influencer marketing is a principle of likeability and authority.

Chapter Two

Influencer marketing is the real gold nugget

Traditional advertising methods are gradually becoming extinct as more businesses prefer influencer marketing method based on the high rate of conversion and effectiveness. From the following statistics, this fact should come as a surprise.

- 74% of consumers prefer to source for a guide to making purchase decisions online
- 86% of online retailers in the United States have Facebook fan pages
- 53% of Twitter users recommend products, services, and companies through tweets
- 48% of consumers deliver on their intention to purchase a product.

Furthermore, a precise study by the Nielsen shows that 90% of consumers across the globe trust peer recommendations. In comparison, a meager 33% of them trust online banner ads.

More so, Adobe and PageFair published a report that showed the increase in ad blocking between the year 2014 and 2015 by about 41% - clearly indicating that traditional methods of advertising may be unreliable in this era.

Presently, statistics show that:

- 65% of brands across the globe participate in influencer marketing
- 52% of companies can brag of a sponsored social budget for their brand
- 25% of companies have an annual budget of $500K while 5% have an organizational annual budget over $5 million.

Meanwhile, influencer marketing comprises several tactics you must be aware of. To make your campaign more active, some marketing strategies fuel influencer marketing.

First, content is vital in influencer marketing campaigns. When partnering with an influencer, you must create content together. While the influencer may come up with the material, the brand may also create a piece that will be featured on the influencer's page.

The second arm is social media. You cannot separate social media component from campaigns. Most influencers will participate in the campaign by sharing a tagline that relates to the campaign. For instance, a health and fitness brand's hashtag for a particular product on social media may be 'fitness tracker.' The influencer will share this content with the suitable hashtag for better penetration and conversion.

Chapter Three

Benefits of influencer marketing in business

Influencer marketing can be of great benefit to your business in unimaginable ways. Regardless of the business size or structure, you should consider this method to amplify your advertising efforts.

Establishment of an audience base: One of the foundational examples of running influencer marketing is to grow the customer base – converting prospective customers into active ones and retaining the active ones as well. It is much easier to sway or persuade the customer since such a person is receptive to the influencer's recommendations already.

Creation of content: What do consumers of a specific product or service want? One thing and that is value for money. An influencer must have the skill to put up engaging and thrilling content that shows the value of the product. The right content can go a long way in promoting products and services. Hence, you will improve your search engine ranking automatically.

Building trust and rapport: At a certain point, the follower base or consumers will trust the influencer whenever they make recommendations for a particular product. The process of earning this trust is complicated. However, trust and rapport exist between both sides, and you can use such a connection to build credibility through the influencer.

Driving engagement: When you tell your brand story through influencers, you connect with the target audience. Subsequently, you can drive engagement by putting up posts frequently.

Market penetration: With influencer marketing, you can reach a broader audience despite marketing to a small group of individuals. Thus, you can minimize costs by choosing the right influencer who in turn boosts your brand's consumer rate.

By working with influencers, you also meet company targets and goals which may include:

- Sales: Customer reviews and endorsements are the most effective means to drive sales and quality leads.

- Brand awareness: New audience will understand your brand and product better.

- Trust: With user-generated content; you develop better brand confidence.

- Education: You can educate a large number of people at once.

- Social following: With the support of social media influencers, you can increase your social following whenever they mention your brand.

- SEO Authority: To boost your search ranking, you may get popular sites to link to you.

- Damage control: You build trust in the audience while reducing negative opinions.

- User-generated content: Whenever you encourage your users to share your content on social media, you raise more awareness. This method is sometimes known as the 'snowball' effect.

Chapter Four

Are brand ambassadors and content marketers the same as influencers?

Frankly, it may be difficult to distinguish between the three terms because of the close relationship them. More so, certain people in the industry often interchange the terms for one another. Theoretically, these terms are similar yet different.

4.11   Content marketing

Content marketing is basically about the creation and distribution of valuable and relevant content. The content aims to attract and abstract a target audience. Therefore, content marketing aims to propel the target audience to take a profitable action – for example, purchase a product. In simpler terms, content marketing is the entire scope of content creation and content distribution to meet business goals.

4.12   Influencer marketing

With influencer marketing, the company works with a prominent figure in the same industry to distribute content about a product. The main aim of the material is to encourage internet users to take a course of action. Instead of the creation of content in content marketing, influencer marketing is concerned with the distribution of content.

In content marketing, you should expect a variety of methods for sharing content to promote content visibility. However, a smart business owner can infuse content marketing with influencer marketing in the process of distribution.

The course of action by online consumers

An online consumer sees a post about someone making recommendations for a particular product or service on the internet – preferably social media. When this happens, it means that the influencer has succeeded in piquing the interest of that consumer. The consumer becomes curious about the product and decides to learn some more. The next step is to go on the influencer's blog. Some examples are Instagram, YouTube,

Twitter, or podcasts. The consumer searches for more information and engages with the content as much as possible.

Then the consumer begins to search for validation and clarification about the specifications of the product including shipping details, price, and availability. However, the consumer finds this on the site of the retailer or brand. If the consumer is satisfied with the overall specifications, he or she orders for the product online or at the physical store. This process involves the interconnection of consumers with a mix of influencer and content marketing.

Another variation of both types of marketing is to nurture brand ambassadors for a particular business. Simply put, a brand ambassador is someone who is a representation of your brand. The brand ambassador speaks about your brand with passion as if the business were theirs. Nevertheless, the brand ambassador may be a fan of your brand or your customer advocate. Brand ambassadors amplify the brand awareness of the business by providing a form of crowd-sourced marketing. The only reason they do this is that of the love and passion they have for a product or service. To promote the relationship of your brand ambassador with both online and offline marketers, the brand has to cultivate and encourage them in monetary or other terms. In other cases, the brand ambassador may perform influencer marketing with little or no efforts from the brand owner.

In this social age, you may not have total control over the brand ambassador. Since they are the modern word-of-mouth, they create unique and personal stories intertwined with some form of visuals to make the product or service more appealing. If possible, the brand owner may boost the campaign by providing the brand ambassador with content. On Instagram, hashtags are the most dynamic methods of sharing and building further support for the product.

Chapter Five

How influencers will help your business

The type of working relationship you cultivate with the influencer will determine the level of help to expect from them. For instance, you will receive less help from an influencer if they are for a distinct influencer marketing campaign. This term is known as influencer outreach or organic approach. More so, the cost will be different.

Influencer outreach involves an influencer who influences your brand for free or at the price of some free products. On the other hand, you will pay a formal influencer a lot of money depending on the influencer's fame, popularity, or followership. Nevertheless, you will reap more benefits from paid influencers.

When you develop an organic relationship with the influencer, there are certain ways the influencer would help your brand.

Creation of blog post, video, or article about a service or product: When they social media shares information about you on their social media accounts, it is a gradual process to influence your followership as well. In other cases, they may share content from your page giving their followers direct access to your page.

Giving you access to personal sites to write a guest post: To promote your brand, the influencer has to be very proactive. Examples of articles are strictly professional content and videos. For a particular product, they may share videos or content about how to use the product. Because they earn money from, they are expected to put in a lot of efforts to ensure that your brand sells.

Also, unequivocal praise for your brand is what you should expect from the influencer. Since they have a strong bond with the audience, they will persuade them to purchase your product or service. Most importantly, influencers may not work with you if they do not like your brand or are already working with a brand in the same niche as yours.

Trends in the influencer marketing business

For several thousands of years, influencer marketing has been in existence in different forms. As far back as Ancient Greek when orators and celebrity endorsers were the real deal to the 19th century, influencer marketers have always been of significant impact to the success of businesses. However, there has been a substantial evolution in the trends and methods for influencer marketing.

In 2015, Marketing Charts published a report which showed that the most effective channels for implementing influencer marketing are guest posts at 69% and events at 70%. In the same report, it seems that more than 67% of brands will gravitate towards influencer marketing to promote products. The reason that businesses also work with influencers is that of the increased popularity of product launches and content creation on blogs.

For several years, the influence of blogs has been a continuous trend. A survey in 2012 by Burst Media shows that blogs are effective in influencing purchase decision of young readers between the age group of 18 to 34. Eight out of ten readers were also motivated to purchase a product due to brand mentions in blog content.

Augure also reported a study which demonstrates that 93% of respondents think that influencer marketing is best for brand recognition and visibility on social media.

Chapter Six

Getting started

If your reason for considering influencer marketing is because it is trendy, you need to change our perspective. A great marketing campaign always begins with a goal and a purpose. Compare this with some other facets of business; you may find no difference. Many successful business persons will tell you that they are winning because of viable goals and plans which are secret ingredients to great businesses.

You must have quality content if your influencer marketing must be successful. However, you will not attract the attention of the influencer with a 500-word blog post whose only criteria is to meet SEO.

To protect your content for better penetration, the content must be:

- Actionable
- Accessible

- Visual appealing

- Provides excellent value to the reader

There are certain ways you can package your content to attract the appeal of the influencer. The content that meets all the criteria listed above should be included in an ideal content such as:

- Interviews

- Listicles

- Expert roundup

- Ask for the experts' tip and string them in one blog post

- Create a SlideShare or ask your selected influencer for a quote and use for infographics

Determine the source of your potential influencer's audience to check out how it matches with your clientele. Also, many influencers have selected places where they make their names for brands to select them. They are:

Blogs: Many bloggers spend several years in building and nurturing a successful brand by constantly engaging a dedicated audience with specific content in a particular niche. In recent years, the most popular fashion influencer gain influence across several platforms. However, the quality of blogs is the foundation of the initial fame of the bloggers. Your best option is to choose quality bloggers, and it can be in several ways.

- Product reviews
- Brand mentions in posts
- Guest posts on a personal blog
- Post sponsorship

Social media: It is difficult to see a celebrity without an account on social media especially Instagram and Twitter. Along with those who run quality blogs, these celebrities have a humongous engagement and following on their accounts. Your aim on the brand should include:

- Shares or retweets of your social media posts
- Receiving positive mentions in social posts

- Posts that show where an influencer uses a particular product or service. For instance, unboxing video on the YouTube channel of the influencer

- Innovative social posts that highlight the promotion of the selected brand

Before you start, you need to make significant decisions. One of such decisions is to determine the best method to abstract influencers. A few options to consider are:

- Agencies: Specialist influencer marketing agencies are critical at this stage. When you pay a particular token, the company will help you with selection and management of influencer.

- Organic: This is the cheapest yet time-consuming method of searching and building a relationship with influencers online.

- Platforms: You can find the influencer by consulting a specialist online platform that is effective in selecting the best influencers. These platforms provide computerized

systems that simplify and manage the influencer campaign.

Chapter Seven

Finding the right influencers by setting goals

Demonstration of the value you can provide to the audience is the goal of a content marketing campaign. For influencer marketing, a brand must show its consumers that they can provide the needed value.

Define your goals

While it may be cliché to assume that 'you should prepare to fail if you fail to prepare,' the saying is very applicable to influencer marketing. Without setting sustainable and achievable goals at the very beginning, there is no point taking on influencer marketing. It is not surprising that a meager 18% of firms without an actionable target for their influencer marketing reaped positive returns from the campaign. If you cannot answer the 'why' of your marketing aspirations, it is a great time to call it quits. Without valid reasons for influencer marketing, how will you measure the success of the campaign? More so, it can blur your chances of selecting the most suitable brand influencer.

Simple goals you can set for your influencer campaigns should be:

- To increase the number of visitors to the website or blog to a particular target percentage
- To increase the number of social media followers of the brand
- To increase the visibility of the brand for a particular audience. For example, Grad DNA chose the influencer marketing option for the need to boost the awareness of the brand name and app using influencers. Their primary target was to achieve about three thousand downloads by students of the campaign.
- To increase sales of product by a certain amount or percentage

The type of influencer you choose will depend on your goals. You are likely to work with influencers who are active on

Twitter if you want quick interaction with people. If you want to emphasize the image and look of your product, you may emphasize a visual channel such as Pinterest or Instagram. If you aim to provide product awareness (in-depth), especially for business to business models, you may opt to post a technical article on a blog. More so, you may have the article's share links.

However, there must be a crucial relatable performance indicator that is binding on the goals. After all, how would it be convenient to measure the campaign's success? If your campaign's goal is to increase sales, for example, you may want to make comparisons of your sales figures before you start the campaign and after. Likewise, you will have a definite KPI you can measure if your goal is to grow sign-ups to your newsletter

Have you heard about SMART goals? It is high time to create SMART goals.

SMART stands for:

S – *Specific*

M – *Measurable*

A – *Achievable*

R – *Realistic*

T – Time-based

You cannot measure the goal of increasing product awareness because it is too vague. Meanwhile, an actionable SMART goal is to 'increase following on Twitter by 30%' during March. More so, it is difficult to determine the success or failure of the influencer.

7.11 Define your target audience

If you do not know who you want your influencers to 'influence,' it is impossible to find the right influencer. At this stage in your business, you should know what your ideal customer looks like. If this is the case, you must create a mental picture of such followers during your search for influencers. To have a successful influencer marketing, you must work with the type of followers that influence your target audience. For example, a particular brand has a huge marketing budget sufficient to work with Selena Gomez as the brand influencer. Selena Gomez is the perfect option if your product is geared towards teenage boys and girls. The same applies to Justin Bieber who has over 100 million followers and a Klout score of 92 and above. However, Justin may be unable to convince his millions of followers to patronize a brand in the furniture business. Therefore, the influencer's supporters are not the ideal target audience for the brand. This is a convenient time to move past Justin to a more suitable public figure.

Hence, you find the right influencers as long as you can narrow your target market down to a specific niche.

7.12 Finding the right influencer for your brand

One of the toughest decisions you will make for your brand is the perfect influencer. To ensure that your product or service gets optimum exposure; you must choose the right influencer. Fortunately, some metrics are essential indicators for evaluating potential influencers.

- Relevance: The chosen influencer must be relevant to your industry if they must significantly impact your target audience. You must verify that they are experts in the industry. Also, you need to examine if their content attracts a relevant audience.

- Reach: To promote your brand, the right candidate must have a certain level of reach. Check out their numbers of social followers. If sufficient, be sure that they have significant social media engagement to achieve your business goals effectively.

- Engagement rate or level of influence: Whenever the candidate shares content, how well do the followers interact and engage with the content? Are these followers or users even sharing or reposting the influencer's content on relevant social channels? Check out the average number of comments that each post generates. Most importantly, is the right candidate well recommended? A good formula to use is Engagement rate $(E)(E\_1 + E\_2 + E\_3)/3$. By representation, E is the number of lies + number of shares + total number of followers. 'E' accounts for three similar types of posts on the social media network. Instagram is one of the social networks where you can remove the number of shares count because there is no such parameter to determine this on the platform. The comparison of 'E' is only valid and relevant to a particular social network at a time. For instance, you cannot compare EFB to ETWITTER or EINSTAGRAM

The influencer has a high probability of influencing a business with a high E. In a case where you are comparing many influencers, the one with the highest E is the perfect candidate for the job. The metrics and formula above help to determine the merit of potential influencers for spreading brand content. But there are other ways to find influencers across several social networking channels.

7.13 Finding influencers on Twitter

Twitter is undeniably the best platform to find the best influencers. With the advanced search option, you can reap several benefits from the social media page. Based on hashtags, key phrases, and words, you can conduct a search based on the influencer. For example, you can type on 'social media' to find the top profiles that match your search item. Then, click on the Twitter tab of the 'Influencer Campaign Template' and add results of the most relevant influencers from the search.

7.14   Finding influencers on LinkedIn

On LinkedIn, you can utilize the 'search by industry' tab. LinkedIn has some location filters to narrow down the brand's most relevant influencers. Based on industries, you have the freedom to filter searches. The concerned industries may be computer software, marketing, and online media. On LinkedIn, you can also search for posts that contain particular keywords. Afterward, you can filter the results depending on the author, post time, and relevance. If you want to connect with prominent influencers within your niche and subsequently connect with them, use LinkedIn today.

When you check out LinkedIn, you will find out that you can track the volume of posts that a LinkedIn user publishes from time to time. Furthermore, check out the prospective candidate's number of followers. They are more likely to be influencers in their community if they have great followership.

Search for LinkedIn's Influencer Campaign Template and click on one tab. Then, add the results of the relevant influencers from your search on LinkedIn. A unique factor to note about each candidate is the number of followers. More so, the average number of comments and likes the user generates from their posts is of utmost importance. With this information, you will successfully make the best selection for your brand amidst tons of prospective candidates.

7.15 Finding influencers on Instagram

On Instagram, the best method is to conduct a Google search. In your industry, there may be some existing files that will help identify top influencers. All you need to do is to search for 'top Instagram accounts' in the Google search tab. Industry-specific terms will help you to streamline your search as well. For instance, brands in the fashion and wellness industries may use 'fashion' and 'fitness' as search terms.

With relevant hashtags, you can also perform an Instagram search. Nevertheless, Iconosquare is a useful tool that helps to unravel the mystery by finding the best influencers through hashtag research. For instance, you will get the top results for a keyword such as 'health and fitness' in Iconosquare. To research the suggested list of influencers, all you have to do is to click on any exciting profile.

Search for Instagram's Influencer Campaign Template and click on one tab. Then, add the results of the relevant influencers from our search on Instagram or Iconosquare. Record essential data such as average likes, the total number of followers, and the number of comments. With this information, you will successfully make the best selection for our brand amidst tons of prospective Instagram influencers.

7.16 Finding influencers on Facebook

Interestingly, it is challenging to find influencers on Facebook. The main reason is due to the number of restrictions on Facebook. Nevertheless, it doesn't mean that it is impossible to find exciting influencers within your niche on this social media channel. Go to the search bar on Facebook and type a term that relates to your business or industry. About the search term, the Facebook result will list some top people and pages that match the search term. To confirm if they will be of use to your influencer marketing campaign, click on specific profiles.

Another useful method to search on Facebook is to use hashtags. When you search with hashtags, you will see top posts from different Facebook users and pages. Again, click on relevant profiles to confirm their relevance to your business, brand, or industry.

Search for Facebook's Influencer Campaign Template. Then, click on a tab to add relevant influencers from your search on Facebook. Check out essential metrics such as the number of shares, average likes, number of followers, and number of post comments.

Chapter Eight

Different types of influencers

There are different types of influencer marketers; making it more difficult to choose one. So many brands fail in aligning the personality of the influencer with that of their brand goals. Hence, the reason why some brands do not meet their targets.

A study bTapinfluence/Altimeter shows that 67.6% of marketers believe that the most substantial influencer marketing challenge is to find the most relevant influencers for their brand. However, it is great to conclude that traditional celebrity marketing saw this as a challenge as well. Even though there are some successes so far, most consumers would want to know what a celebrity (influencer) feels about their lifestyle. Thus, the influencer and the target audience must have a confluence point at which they share similar ideas and likes.

8.11   What are the types of influencers?

Even though the boundaries may be unclear, there are majorly three sets of influencers that will be great for an influencer campaign.

Celebrity influencers

This is the oldest style of influencer marketing. For several years, many prominent brands have boosted their sales and followership by hiring competent celebrities that endorse their products. An example of a favorite brand is George Foreman Grill whose popularity is linked to the celebrity with which it shares a name. Both traditional and modern online types of celebrity campaigns have a high rate of success. Spectrum Brands, the owner of the George Foreman Grill brand, paid George Foreman to provide his name and image for the grill. The marketing campaign was a significant boost to the company's profit base. Till date, many people recognize the brand as 'George Foreman' and not Spectrum Brands.

On the other hand, several problems would arise from working with a celebrity. It is not surprising that many celebrities would be very expensive. For instance, a brand would pay Kim Kardashian about $250, 000 for posting a single picture of her on Instagram.

Also, consumers are always finicky about celebrities who endorse brands that they do not use. If there is a discrepancy between the influencer and the target market, the brand may not generate a lot of sales after spending thousands of dollars to the influencer to promote that brand. For instance, Kim Kardashian may not pull off a 'home renovation' advert because most people in that niche wouldn't expect her to know a lot about home renovations. More so, she may not be influential enough to change the buying behavior on promoting the brand.

Nevertheless, this may not be a significant problem where the consumer believes in the genuineness of the influencer. There are several cases where a celebrity has been a significant change in the fashion trend because of what they wore at the Golden Globe Awards or the Met Gala. For example, there was a time when Emma Watson was caught on camera spotting a scarf from British knitwear company – Crumpet. From the photograph, there was no mistake that she was passionate about the scarf. In less than three weeks, Crumpet made about 62% increases in sales from a minute influence from the celebrity. Also, Kate Middleton was the reason a particular maternity dress was sold out in minutes after her photograph in the dress surfaced on the internet. These are mere e examples of what is happening in the real world of celebrity influencers. By choosing that perfect celebrity, you never know what you may get.

Macro influencers

By inference, macro influencers are people with a colossal following. Because of the number of followers, they are seen as experts in the field. On various social networks combined, they often have millions of followers. The tag 'expert' is the only term that distinguishes a macro influencer from a celebrity. For example, the global rating of the top three influencers according to Onalytica in the content marketing field includes Neil Patel, Joe Pulizzi, and Jeff Bullas. Their influencer scores according to Onalytica are 83.79, 96.83, and 100.00 respectively.

On Twitter, these top three influencers have followings such as:

Jeff Bullas – 562, 000 followers

Joe Pulizzi – 141, 000 followers

Neil Patel – 284, 000 followers

These three men are superstars of their niche when you add other social media channels with their influential blogs.

However, these people aren't celebrities. When you ask an average person on the street, they may not even have heard about them before. They are macro-influencers and not celebrities. You will get more returns on investment when you work with any of these content marketing gurus if content marketing is your niche. And who knows? You may pay lesser than what you have to pay a celebrity that is unlikely to meet your business goals.

As long as macro-influencers are concerned, these people are thought leaders and industry experts. They include professional and academics advisors and journalists in their ranks.

Nevertheless, there are specific problems with macro-influencers as you will find with celebrities. The truth is that macro-influencers have made a name for themselves. In most cases, they rank high in their field, and the income is a reflection of that. A macro-influencer may work with a brand for two reasons:

Provision of massive incentive for the influencer to work with

Genuine love for your product or service. A brand can benefit from an organic relationship with the macro-influencer. If they love our product, service, or content, they may be happy to share posts.

Micro influencers

Micro-influencers make up the most significant bulk of influencers. In simple terms, they may be scaled-down versions. Contrary to celebrities, they do not have widespread fame in their niche. However, people who know them in their niche refer to them as experts.

In niche topics, micro influencers are the people who are on top of their game – especially in topics that are not very popular. On the other hand, they are experts in niche subjects but never the ones at the top. Most times, they are often below the macro influencers on the pyramid of influencers. Therefore, micro influencers are the best alternatives when a brand had an influencer marketing campaign. More than the average person, they have a significant support base but not as large to be so wealthy or busy to disregard offers for influencer campaigns.

Again, micro influencers may lack reasonable following – most are in the range of 500 to 10, 000 followers. Besides, they engender a high level of engagement. The recognition of their knowledge on specialist topics is well-known to the followers, hence making the followers' die-hard fans.

Also, many micro influencers have a great interest in purchasing products or services. According to research by Expercity/The Keller Fay Group, they have 22.2 times more conversations weekly about reviews and recommendations on what to buy compared to average consumers. Bloglovin' also claims that 53% of micro-influencers receive frequent payments for the promotion of a post. This step is not necessary. Because of the strong bond and rapport between the influencer and the followers, word of mouth and organic reach are enough to persuade the follower to purchase the product.

When you work with the perfect influencer, you will attract customers that are important to your business goals.

Never make fame be the reason or foundation for choosing a specific influencer. Also, do not work with an influencer because they will charge you less.

One thing that should be at the core of your mind is that you are looking for an influencer that has a strong support base who will target the right audience that our brand needs. In simple words, your influencer's fans are your fans.

Your marketing campaign has a high rate of success when you find these influencers.

In addition to the above points, do not judge the perfect influencer by the number of followers they have. It is common practice for some dishonest influencers to buy followers. Even when the number of followers is genuine, it is not a useful guide to the level of influence of the person. The perfect influencer is the one with a reasonable number of highly engaged followers.

As the number of followers increases, the rate of engagement tends to fall by a certain percentage. You must balance people with reasonable engagement and huge followings, with influencers with active engagement and moderate following. A logical approach may be in the selection of the influencer with the broadest reach. But a brand tends to gain a better conversion from the influencer with a smaller following.

8.12   Brand ambassadors

These are also forms of micro-influencers. However, brand ambassadors are self-appointed micro influencers. They promote your product if and when they like it without involving you. Your unofficial brand ambassador is one of the few people that will promote your product with passion and enthusiasm. They upload visuals of the product or success stories of the service. A perfect example of brand ambassadors is people who pin images on Pinterest boards for the love of a product.

Most times, these self-appointed brand ambassadors turn out to become active figures in the marketing campaign of the brand. An excellent place to start from is to provide free products to the most responsive and fervent supporters or followers. You can also start a competition where you urge them to use hashtags of the product or service for a cash prize or incentive.

Chapter Nine

Top Tools to find great influencers

Manually, it is tough to find influencers. While you are burning productive hours of your business in searching for one, you are also losing money. Fortunately, the Internet of Things shows some useful tools that can make your search for a great influencer faster and more effective.

Little Bird

This is a handy tool that unravels the number of reliable influencers with validations from people on Twitter. From the search list, you will get several specialists from which you can choose the one that matches your brand needs. By using engagement tools on the app, you can also connect and start a chat with favorite influencers.

FollowerWonk

This is a Twitter analytics tool which is very useful in selecting the right influencers for a specific brand. By using specific keywords, you can search for people that are relevant to the business goals. Also, the tool ranks the results based on social authority and reach. For each profile that comes up, you can view the number of followers and tweets. To better understand the influencer's reach, you will find a tool that displays the social authority of the influencer. Interestingly, this tool can aid your selection b highlighting the probability that a particular influencer may be a prospective candidate.

BuzzSumo

This tool searches for the most popular content that relates to a specific topic. The aim is to identify the content authors with significant influence. Keywords and hashtags are also active on this platform for searching for influencers. More so, search filters will help to sort your influencer option based on journalists, bloggers, types, and companies. Check out the domain authority and page authority that the influencer has. Some other information you will find on BuzzSumo includes reply ratio, average retweets, and retweet ratio which are useful tools for selecting the right influencer.

Traackr

This tool is more industry-specific. It helps a brand uncover a list of influencers that are the perfect authority figure in that industry. Profiles, dynamic lists, sentiment analysis, and trending content are features you will find on Traackr. For easy searching, you can sort your results by influencer rank.

Kred

This is another Twitter tool that evaluates replies, mentions, retweets and follows. What better way to find influencer marketers than this? To know whether the influencer will likely forward other people's content; the tool provides outreach activity of the influencer. Thus, you will focus on the types of influencers that are beneficial to you alone.

Keyhole

This Instagram hashtag-tracking tool helps to discover influencers and content with specific hashtags. You will find individuals who are leading industry-related events, conversations, and topics. Keyhole also reveals the number of followers and level of exposure of a particular influencer. Hence, you will see the candidates with the most influence in the industry.

Mention

Mention is a straight-forward tool that highlights the number of people that are sharing and supporting your brand. By using their influencer score, you can select the most influential of the bulk of people.

PeerIndex

PeerIndex is another innovative tool that tracks influencers based on the ability to drive engagement and action. Contrary to several tools, its focus is beyond follower count. To measure a person's influence, it uses the expertise of the individual.

Klout

You will find some influencers based on selected topics. The primary motive of the tool is to search for people with the highest social influence. You can get an overview of people in our industry by looking them up in Klout.

Chapter Ten

How to pitch an influencer

An Augure survey shows that 66% of respondents will contact prospective influencers through email. Other active channels for contacting influencers are Twitter and blogs which have a success rate of 57% and 52% respectively.

There are a few ways to find the email address of the influencer before you begin our email influencer outreach.

Some influencers will add their email address to their bio. Thus, checking social media accounts for substantial email information may be a great start.

You can use Google to search for the name of the influencer and their email platform.

Data.com – this tool efficiently accesses the email address information of potential influencers.

Ninja Outreach – this tool shows the contact details of potential influencers.

If the potential influencer has a personal domain, use Domain Tools to search for their email address.

The most preferred influencer outreach channel is email. Here is a particular template that is important in pitching to potential influencers. However, you can customize the templates as much as possible.

For instance:

Hey [influencer],

My name is [...] from [company]. I've been an avid follower of your blog since 2012. I was especially intrigued by your latest post on [topic].

I know that you're quite selective about doing promotions, so I'm only reaching out to you regarding a product I believe would be of great benefit to your audience.

It's a [product], which many of your readers will find useful to [benefits/uses of product].

We're looking to partner with a select few individuals to provide their email subscribers with a special limited time offer. You will get an X% share of the profit.

If you're interested, we can schedule a call next week to discuss the details.

Regards,

Hope

Chapter Eleven

The future of influencer marketing

The future of influencer marketing is bright and promising. Because it is a solution to many traditional marketing methods' problems, expect more brands to adopt the method soon enough. For example, banner blindness with online marketing and audience fragmentation with online marketing.

In several methods, influencer marketing is on the rise and wouldn't cease to rise. It is relatively new to the market and is very innovative. Therefore, there is still a lot to discover about influencer marketing than we have all the answers to.

Several years ago, influencer marketing was not an option. It didn't even exist. Some celebrities would promote products offline and be considered as the closest tactic to the scope of influencer marketing in the present day. Also, web owners did not know about the real worth of websites because social networks such as Facebook were not widespread. None of them realized the amount of power they possess over an audience. More so, brands had no idea about these people.

In the previous years, these influencers did not know the degree of value of their audience – their online asset. Also, people had worried that having a phone close to the ears for some time would mean radiation poison. Strict parents would discourage their offspring from signing up on social media accounts. Even the parents were not active users of social media.

However, there is a new story on everyone's lips. A specific influencer can boast of millions of followers on social media account. Interestingly, various websites suit different niches in the industry – parenting, kids, and social environments for the aged. Furthermore, farmers spend hours online to compare weather and agricultural data while researching the best products that would be suitable.

Also, several followers hold top social media influencers in awe; others are diehard fans. It is for this reason that actors, elite musicians, and sportspeople. Luckily, the story will not change anytime soon. Check out how kids spend time with some things and are sure of the heroes they claim to have.

Conclusion

The shift from traditional marketing to digital marketing is tremendous. However, this movement has had its fair share of opportunities and challenges. In an attempt to reach new customers online, brands are focusing on the younger generation and audience.

Influencer marketing is swiftly replacing traditional adverts since social media, and digital influencers are impacting purchase decisions in this generation.

Don't be left behind in this new age of influencer marketing. An increasing number of businesses are employing smarter ways to increase their conversions and in the end, profit. The methods and tools in this eBook will lay the foundation of your strategies to promote your brand with the help of top influencers.

www.ingramcontent.com/pod-product-compliance
Lightning Source LLC
Chambersburg PA
CBHW030734180526
45157CB00008BA/3157